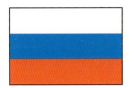  

Flags

By
Maureen Dockendorf
and Sharon Jeroski

CELEBRATION PRESS
Pearson Learning Group

The following people from **Pearson Learning Group**
have contributed to the development of this product:

Joan Mazzeo, Dorothea Fox **Design** | **Editorial** Leslie Feierstone Barna, Teri Crawford Jones
Christine Fleming **Marketing** | **Publishing Operations** Jennifer Van Der Heide
Production Laura Benford-Sullivan
Content Area Consultant Dr. Daniel J. Gelo

The following people from **DK** have
contributed to the development of this product:

Art Director Rachael Foster
Martin Wilson **Managing Art Editor** | **Managing Editor** Marie Greenwood
Sarah Crouch **Design** | **Editorial** Hannah Wilson
Helen McFarland **Picture Research** | **Production** Gordana Simakovic
Richard Czapnik, Andy Smith **Cover Design** | **DTP** David McDonald
Consultant Philip Wilkinson

Dorling Kindersley would like to thank: Rose Horridge in the DK Picture Library; Ed Merrit and Simon Mumford for cartography; and Johnny Pau for additional cover design work.

Picture Credits: Alamy Images: Steve Allen 1c; Jan Baks 13br; Chris Bellentine 4tl; Michael Grant 18tl; Chris Jackson 4cla; Bragi Thor Josefsson/Nordicphotos.com 27cl; Pictor International/Imagestate 4b, 8bl; Popperfoto 29c. Associated Press AP: Stringer 15tr, 28bc. Bridgeman Art Library, London/New York: Bibliotheqee Nationale, Paris 6tr. © The British Museum: 5t. Corbis: 19t, 28cr; Dean Conger 18b; Historical Picture Archive 20bl; Michale S. Lewis 28bl; Galen Rowell 8cr, 28tr; Pascal Le Segretain /SYGMA 7tr; Wendy Stone 29cl; Michael S. Yamashita 9cr. Mary Evans Picture Library: Explorer/ADPC 11b. Werner Forman Archive: Museum fur Volkerkunde, Basel 17tr. Getty Images: Doug Armand 24br;Tony Feder/Allsport 22cr. NASA: Jacques Descloitres, MODIS Rapid Response Team, NASA/GSFC 14bl. Pa Photos: EPA 29br.
Cover: Alamy Images: Brian Lawrence/Imagestate front t. Getty Images: Tony Feder/Allsport back.

All other images: DK Dorling Kindersley © 2005. For further information see www.dkimages.com

Text Copyright © 2005 Pearson Education, Inc., publishing as Celebration Press, a division of Pearson Learning Group. Compilation Copyright © 2005 Dorling Kindersley Ltd. All rights reserved. No part of this book may be reproduced or transmitted in any form or by any means, electronic or mechanical, including photocopying, recording, or any information storage and retrieval system, without permission in writing from the proprietors.

For information regarding licensing and permissions, write to Rights and Permissions Department, Pearson Learning Group, 299 Jefferson Road, Parsippany, NJ 07054 USA or to Rights and Permissions Department, DK Publishing, The Penguin Group (UK), 80 Strand, London WC2R 0RL.

Lexile is a U.S. registered trademark of MetaMetrics, Inc. All rights reserved.

ISBN: 0-7652-5249-X

Color reproduction by Colourscan, Singapore
Printed and bound in China by Leo Paper Products Ltd.
1 2 3 4 5 6 7 8 9 10   08 07 06 05 04

1-800-321-3106
www.pearsonlearning.com

Contents

Flags Are Flying	4
Flags of Many Colors	8
The Symbols on Flags	13
Changing Flags	20
International Flags	24
Flag Customs and Traditions	27
Flags of the World	30
Index	32

Flags Are Flying

A flag may look like a brightly colored piece of cloth, but it is actually much more than that. A flag can identify a nation. It can be an important symbol, standing for the beliefs, hopes, and dreams of the people who wave it. A flag can be used to rally people to a common cause. A flag can sometimes tell a story.

Flags are made to be seen, so most are large pieces of cloth that light breezes can blow.

Colors, patterns, and designs make each country's flag unique.

Ancient Flags

No one knows exactly what the first flag looked like or who used it. Many early societies used flags to identify themselves and to signal from a distance.

In ancient Egypt, warriors carried fans and carvings high on poles to identify themselves. Roman soldiers carried objects, often with small pieces of cloth attached, which identified their army units. In China and India, flags represented rulers or kings. In some cultures, flags carried such symbolism that if a flag fell in battle, it was as if the leader had been killed.

This ancient Egyptian pot shows a very early form of a flag on the top right.

Ancient Assyrians, from the area now called the Middle East, carried carved symbols on poles. These standards, which were carried into battle, were early forms of flags.

This is a modern reconstruction of an ancient Roman flag.

Flags of the Middle Ages

In the Middle Ages, cities, countries, and even powerful people used flags to identify themselves. Crosses, crescents, trefoils (symbols based on flowers or herbs with three leaves), lions, falcons, unicorns, and dragons were sewn onto colored fabric. These images were symbols that displayed information about the people who carried them. In battle, soldiers could recognize friends and enemies from a distance. If a city was captured, a flag was raised over its walls to identify the new ruler.

This medieval artwork shows a battle scene from the Hundred Years' War between France and England, which began in 1337. The artwork shows flags being carried into battle on horseback.

Pennants and Pennons

Flags come in many shapes, each with a special name. There are rectangular, triangular, and square flags. A few have tails or fringes. Pennants are flags that are much longer than they are wide. They are usually triangular. Pennons are also long and thin, but they often divide into two at the end.

British army pennons were hung from lances.

This old Chinese pennant flew on boats.

Flags of Different Nations

Today, most of the world is divided into nations, and all nations have their own flags. Some of these flags were created hundreds of years ago. Others were designed recently. All the flags represent ideas or values that are important to that nation.

National flags are waved proudly at international gatherings to identify a country.

Many flags reflect their nation's past. They contain colors or patterns that represent important events in a nation's history. Others reflect the geography of a nation, its natural features, and its people. Some flags display symbols that stand for the beliefs, customs, and culture, or way of life, of the people.

The following chapters explore many different national flags. If you are unsure where a particular country is in the world, turn to pages 30 and 31 to find out.

National Flag Shapes

Kuwait

Nepal

Switzerland

Most modern national flags are rectangular, such as Kuwait's flag. Nepal's flag is unusual because it's made of two joined triangles. Switzerland's flag is different from most flags because it is square.

Flags of Many Colors

National flags come in a rainbow of colors that are bold and easy to see from a distance. They are usually arranged in simple patterns that help people recognize the flag instantly. The colors represent things that are important to the people of each nation.

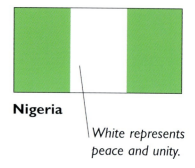

Nigeria

White represents peace and unity.

Colors of Nature

Green often symbolizes nature. The flag of Nigeria is green and white. A student, Michael Taiwo Akinkunmi, designed this flag to honor the fields and forests of his country. In 1958, his flag was chosen from almost 3,000 entries in a competition.

Brazil also has a flag with green on it, representing the lush rain forests covering much of that country. Yellow or gold can represent many things. Ukraine's flag has a yellow stripe that represents wheat fields.

Brazil is home to the Amazon rain forest.

Brazil

The yellow diamond represents Brazil's mineral resources.

Blue represents the sky.

Yellow represents wheat fields.

Ukraine

Many island countries, such as the Bahamas, have blue on their flags to represent the sea that surrounds them. Other countries use blue to represent the sky, whereas others see blue as a color of peace.

Red may represent blood, or the sacrifice people made to fight for their country's independence. Red is also used to represent a number of different political or religious beliefs.

White sometimes represents ice or snow. That is its meaning on the flag of Finland, a country in the far north. However, white also represents ideals such as hope, love, freedom, or peace.

Often, you need to know the story behind a flag to discover what a color symbolizes. The five colors in the flag of Seychelles have symbolic meanings.

Bahamas

Yellow represents the sandy beaches of the Bahamas.

Finland

White represents snow and ice.

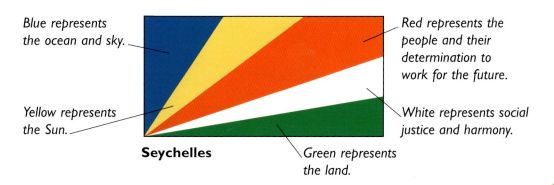

Seychelles

Blue represents the ocean and sky.

Yellow represents the Sun.

Red represents the people and their determination to work for the future.

White represents social justice and harmony.

Green represents the land.

Historic Colors

Some flag colors tell a story about a country's history. In 1785, the king of Spain adopted red and yellow for the national flag. This color combination was not used by any other nation, so it was easy to distinguish Spain's ships from those of other countries.

Spain

The flag of the Netherlands also tells a story of its history. More than 400 years ago, Spain controlled the Netherlands. Prince William of Orange, one of the Dutch leaders, raised an army to help drive the Spanish out. After winning their freedom, the people of the Netherlands adopted an orange, white, and blue flag, similar to Prince William's personal flag. Eventually, the orange stripe was changed to red. To this day, the Netherlands' flag honors William's place in the country's history.

William of Orange

Netherlands

The Netherlands' flag is a tricolor, which means that it has three equal-sized stripes of three colors.

The French flag is also red, white, and blue. Although the colors are the same as the Dutch flag, the history of this flag is different. White was the color of the kings of France, while blue and red were the colors of the capital city of Paris.

In the late 1700s, many people in Paris were starving, while the king and members of the ruling class used France's wealth for themselves. The French people began a revolution to rid France of the king. In 1792, the people overthrew the king, and a new French government was started. Since then, red, white, and blue have represented liberty to people around the world.

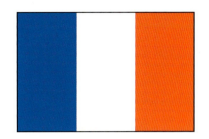

France

The French Revolution began on July 14, 1789, when the people of Paris stormed the Bastille prison.

Some nations chose their flag colors or designs because they were inspired by other nations. The red, white, and blue horizontal stripes of the Russian Federation flag are an example of this. Peter the Great, an emperor of Russia who lived from 1672 to 1725, traveled to the Netherlands and brought its ideas back to Russia. He started schools, built a navy, and even made people dress differently. Although the colors of the Dutch flag had been used for many years, Peter the Great made the horizontal stripes a feature of his own nation's flag.

Paraguay's flag is also red, white, and blue. During the nineteenth century, Paraguay fought for independence from Spain. Inspired by the French Revolution, the people of Paraguay used the colors of the French flag.

Peter the Great

Russian Federation

Paraguay

The colors of Paraguay's flag were taken from the French flag. There is a different emblem on the front and the back of the flag.

State Arms on front of flag

Treasury Seal on back of flag

The Symbols on Flags

Simple bands of color make up the design of many national flags. Other flags have special symbols. These symbols represent important natural features, religious or historic ideas, or cultural traditions.

Symbols of Nature

Lebanon has a cedar tree on its flag. Known as the cedar of Lebanon, this tree has been an important part of Lebanon's history. It provided wood and cedar oil for many ancient civilizations.

The flag of Kiribati, an island nation in the Pacific Ocean, has six wavy bands of blue and white on it. These bands represent the ocean waves. A Sun symbol rises from the waves. Above the Sun is a frigate bird.

Lebanon — cedar tree

Kiribati

The frigate bird is found all over the Pacific.

Stars

Many flags have stars on them. Sometimes these stars represent specific stars or constellations. Flags of some countries in the southern hemisphere, including Australia, New Zealand, and Papua New Guinea, feature a constellation known as the Southern Cross. For centuries, sailors sailing in the southern oceans have used this constellation to guide them.

On Cape Verde's flag, the ten stars represent the ten main islands that make up the country.

Southern Cross Constellation

bird of paradise

Papua New Guinea

Cape Verde

The islands of Cape Verde lie in the Atlantic Ocean, off the coast of west Africa.

New Zealand

The Southern Cross constellation on New Zealand's flag forms a diamond shape.

China

Stars can represent ideas as well. China's flag has five stars. One star is larger than the others and represents communism, a form of government. The Communist Party is the country's governing body. The smaller stars represent groups of people in the country, such as workers and peasants.

The flag of Guinea-Bissau has a black star. This represents freedom and respect for African people.

The star is also a symbol that shows the important role religion plays in many cultures. A star and crescent Moon can be found on flags from many nations where Islam is an important religion. The cross, a Christian symbol, can also be found on many flags.

People in China often hang flags from their apartment blocks to celebrate Chinese National Day.

Guinea-Bissau

A gold star and crescent Moon are traditional symbols for Muslim people.

Fourteen red and white stripes represent the fourteen states of Malaysia.

Malaysia

Historic Symbols

Many flags tell the history of a country. Some designs represent an important event, such as when a country became independent. Others use symbols from much earlier cultures and times. Argentina's flag does both.

The symbol of the Sun at the center of Argentina's flag celebrates the culture of the Incas, Native Americans of Peru, Argentina, and other countries of modern-day South America. The Sun of May on the Argentinean flag represents pride in the Inca culture and also celebrates Argentina's independence from Spain in May, 1816.

Early civilizations are represented on other flags, too. The Cambodian flag displays the image of Angkor Wat, an ancient temple built almost 1,000 years ago.

Argentina

The Sun of May symbol is part of Argentina's flag.

Cambodia

Angkor Wat, a temple in Cambodia, is depicted on the nation's flag.

Mexico

Arms of Mexico

Mexico's flag has an image of an eagle sitting on a cactus eating a snake. This image celebrates a legend of the Aztecs, who are also native peoples of the Americas.

Some flags show the traditional weapons of nations of the past. Swaziland's flag has the image of a shield, a staff, and two spears. The shield and staff are decorated with the images of feathers from local birds. These symbols represent the fight for independence as well as the traditions of the people of Swaziland.

Flags that celebrate people of the past show how much countries everywhere value their history.

This Aztec stone carving has been dated to 1325. The carving shows the eagle of Aztec legend.

Swaziland

Swazi shields are usually made from cow hides.

Poles are put through rows of slits to make shields rigid.

Some people in Kyrgyzstan still live in yurts.

A symbol representing a yurt is found on the flag of Kyrgyzstan.

Kyrgyzstan

The Sun symbol has forty rays. Each ray represents one of the forty Kyrgyz tribes.

Cultural traditions are also represented on flags. From ancient times, the Kyrgyz (KIR-gihz) people were nomads. They moved from place to place in search of grazing land for their animals. The Kyrgyz people lived in yurts, or felt tents. Though life has changed for most Kyrgyz, the yurt is still an important part of their culture. It is represented within a yellow Sun symbol on the flag of Kyrgyzstan (kir-gih-STAN).

Turkmenistan has a long tradition of carpet-making. People weave the complex patterns of the carpets by hand.

Turkmenistan

A stripe on the flag of Turkmenistan represents traditional carpet designs.

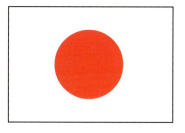

Japan

The Sun rises over Wakayama's rocky coastline in Japan.

Japan's flag, a white field with a red circle in the center, celebrates nature, history, and religion. *Japan* means "Land of the Rising Sun" and the red circle represents the Sun. The emperor of Japan comes from a family that traditionally was said to have descended from a Sun goddess and the red Sun symbol celebrates that connection, as well.

Circles don't always represent the Sun. The red circle on the flag from Bangladesh represents the blood lost in its fight for independence. The yellow circle on the flag from Palau represents the Moon and stands for peace. The people of Palau believe that the full Moon is the best time for harvesting, fishing, and celebration.

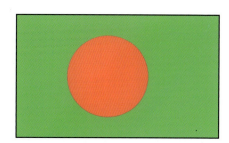

Bangladesh

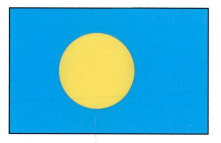

Palau

19

Changing Flags

Nations change over time. Their borders can move because of new agreements between countries or war. Different governments come to power because of new laws or revolution. When nations change, their flags may change, too.

Afghanistan
A new flag was adopted by Afghanistan after the ruling Taliban fell from power in 2001.

The Union Jack

The United Kingdom is made up of England, Northern Ireland, Scotland, and Wales. Its flag, the Union Flag, also known as the Union Jack, is a combination of the flags of three of the four countries.

In 1603, King James of Scotland became king of England, too. Each country kept its own flag, but the new kingdom flew flags from its ships that combined both designs. In the 1800s, Ireland became part of the United Kingdom. One of its flags at the time, a red diagonal cross on white, was added to the United Kingdom's flag. Wales was united with England in the 1500s, but its flag design, which includes a red dragon, is not part of the Union Jack.

United Kingdom
A "jack" is a small flag that is flown on the bow, or front, mast of a ship. In the 1600s, an early version of the Union Jack was flown from ships.

The Union Jack and Other Nations

For many centuries, the United Kingdom explored the world and established settlements, or colonies, on different continents. Today, most of these colonies are independent nations. Some, such as Canada, South Africa, and India, have flags based on traditional designs or symbols that were important before British rule. Other nations, such as Australia, New Zealand, and Fiji, continue to include a Union Jack in one corner.

Canada became divided over the issue of a new national flag in the early 1960s. Canadian Prime Minister Lester B. Pearson called for a new flag to be designed with a symbol specific to Canada.

The maple tree, with its sweet sap and valuable wood, has been important to people living in Canada for hundreds of years. When Canada introduced its new national flag in 1965, a red maple leaf was included in the middle white band. Red and white are the national colors of Canada.

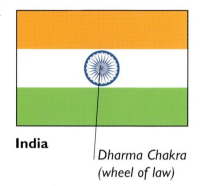

India

Dharma Chakra (wheel of law)

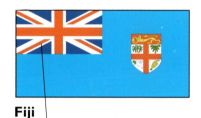

Fiji

The Union Jack represents Fiji's historical links with the United Kingdom.

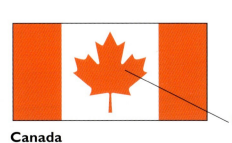

maple leaf

Canada

Australia was once part of the British Empire. Its flag has a Union Jack in the canton, or the upper corner nearest the flagpole. Beneath the Union Jack is a seven-pointed star that represents the six states and the territories that make up Australia. The Southern Cross constellation appears on the fly, or the outer edge of the flag.

Different groups of people within a country often have their own flag to represent themselves. The original inhabitants, or the indigenous peoples, of Australia are the Aboriginal and Torres Strait Islander peoples. They officially adopted their black, gold, and red flag in 1972.

Australia

Aboriginal flag

Cathy Freeman, an indigenous Australian athlete, celebrated a victory with both the Australian and Aboriginal flags.

The Parts of a Flag

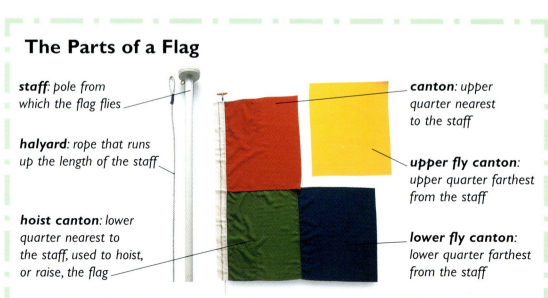

staff: pole from which the flag flies

halyard: rope that runs up the length of the staff

hoist canton: lower quarter nearest to the staff, used to hoist, or raise, the flag

canton: upper quarter nearest to the staff

upper fly canton: upper quarter farthest from the staff

lower fly canton: lower quarter farthest from the staff

The flag of the United States also used to include a Union Jack. This flag, known as the Continental Colors or the Grand Union flag, had thirteen red and white stripes that represented the union of the thirteen original British colonies.

As the American colonies moved toward independence from the United Kingdom, different flags were used for the new country. In 1777, the Continental Congress passed the first Flag Act. This act created a flag that had thirteen stripes, alternating between red and white, and a blue field with thirteen stars. This was the first version of the Stars and Stripes.

Although no one knows for sure, most historians believe that Francis Hopkinson designed this version of the Stars and Stripes flag. There is a legend that Betsy Ross, a seamstress in Philadelphia made the first flag, but most facts do not support this story.

The United States flag kept changing as more states joined the union. At first, a stripe and a star was added for each new state. Later it was decided to keep thirteen stripes, for the original thirteen colonies. Stars were added to show how many states there are. The last star was added in 1960 when Hawaii became a state.

The Union Jack was a symbol of the colonists' loyalty to the United Kingdom.

Grand Union flag

first Stars and Stripes

Fifty stars represent the number of states in the US today.

United States

International Flags

People say the world is getting smaller. It is easier to travel from country to country than ever before. Citizens of one country do business with people from other countries every day, and it is common for people to work or travel in other countries.

Uniting Nations

Many international organizations have formed to help different nations interact. These organizations have flags to identify themselves and their member countries.

United Nations (UN)

The United Nations (UN) is an international organization made up of many nations from all around the world. It was organized to keep the world peaceful and to help resolve emergencies and disagreements between nations.

The flag of the United Nations is pale blue, which stands for peace. The flag shows a white map of the world surrounded by olive branches, ancient symbols of peace and harmony.

The UN's headquarters in New York, United States, has flags from member nations flying outside.

Some international flags represent the union of countries in specific regions of the world. The European Union (EU) is an international organization made up of countries in Europe. The countries cooperate economically, reduce trade barriers, and most use the same currency.

European Union (EU)

The Arab League represents Middle Eastern countries such as Saudi Arabia, Kuwait, and Lebanon. A gold chain on the Arab League's green flag represents the unity of the countries.

Arab League

The Association of Southeast Asian Nations (ASEAN) encourages countries such as Singapore, Malaysia, and Thailand to work together. Its flag includes a design representing ten rice stalks. Each stalk represents one of the ten member nations. The blue background of the flag represents peace and stability.

Association of Southeast Asian Nations (ASEAN)

The Caribbean Community and Common Market (CARICOM) was founded in 1973. Countries that are members include the Bahamas and Jamaica.

Dark blue represents the sea.

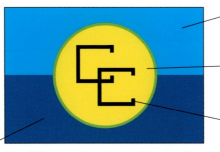
Caribbean Community and Common Market (CARICOM)

Light blue represents the sky.

The yellow circle represents the Sun.

The black letters are the initials of the Caribbean Community.

More International Flags

The Red Cross and the Red Crescent flags represent international groups that bring health care and emergency relief to people all over the world. The flags are symbols of peace and care, but they are also signals. The organization's workers are often in dangerous locations, including war zones. The flags signal that the workers have no part in the conflict.

The flag of the Olympic Games displays five interlocking rings representing the union of athletes from five parts of the world—Africa, the Americas, Asia, Australia, and Europe.

Some flags don't relate to an organization, but have meanings that are understood worldwide. A plain white flag often means truce, or surrender. A yellow flag warns of disease.

Red Crescent

Red Cross

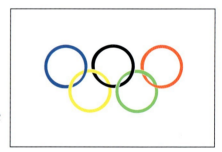
Olympic Games

Jolly Roger

A white skull and crossed bones or swords on a black background is familiar as the flag of pirate ships.

Flag Customs and Traditions

Citizens of all nations treat their flags with respect. In fact, most countries have laws to ensure that they do so. Respecting the flag means different things in different countries, however.

This Icelandic flag is flying at half-mast, a sign of respect and sorrow about the death of an important person.

Respecting the Flag

Citizens in some countries believe the flag should not be dipped in salute to any person. It definitely should never touch the ground. In other countries, however, dipping a flag is a common sign of respect.

In some countries, it is also disrespectful to write on the flag. In other countries, this is not considered disrespectful at all. For example, in Argentina, 750 people who gave money to help World War I soldiers signed their names on a decorative Argentinean flag.

During World War II, some Japanese soldiers carried national flags into battle that had prayers and good wishes from their families written on them. The prayers were never written over the red Sun symbol.

Flags in Exploration

It is a tradition to erect a flag to mark a great feat of exploration. Mountaineers, astronauts, and adventurers have left their flag at their final destination, wherever that may be.

The erection of a flag does not mean that a particular nation owns the place. Roald Amundsen planted the Norwegian flag on the South Pole on December 14, 1911, but this doesn't mean that the South Pole belongs to Norway.

The flags of many countries fly at the South Pole. They represent explorers who reached the Pole.

There is no atmosphere on the Moon—so no wind. Flags in space are often specially wired or hung from a horizontal bar to look like they are fluttering in the breeze.

Appa Sherpa (left) of Nepal and Gheorghe Dijmarescu of the United States display the Nepalese flag on the summit of Mount Everest.

Flags and Fun

Flags are important national symbols, but that doesn't stop them from being fun. They are flown at festivals all over the world, giving people the chance to celebrate their own country and to learn about others.

Flags can decorate everything from clothes and bags to mugs and plates. Sometimes the whole flag design is printed onto objects, and other times just the colors are borrowed to represent a particular nation.

Flags play a huge role in international sporting events. Spectators cheer on their national team and show support by waving their nation's flag.

These Norwegian soccer fans have painted their faces with the colors of Norway's flag.

At this National Festival of Youth in Burundi, school groups perform traditional dances and songs under their national flag (center).

The tallest supported flagpole in the world is in North Korea. It soars 525 feet into the sky.

Flags of the World

There are more than 190 countries in the world, and all of them have their own national flag. Here, we show the location of the countries whose flags we have explored in this book.

Index

Aboriginal flag 22
Afghanistan 20
Arab League 25
Argentina 16, 27
Association of Southeast Asian
    Nations (ASEAN) 25
Assyrians, ancient 5
Australia 14, 21, 22, 26
Aztecs 17
Bahamas 9, 25
Bangladesh 19
Brazil 8
Burundi 29
Cambodia 16
Canada 21
Cape Verde 14
Caribbean Community and
    Common Market (CARICOM) 25
China 5, 15
Egypt, ancient 5
European Union (EU) 25
Fiji 21
Finland 9
France 11
Guinea-Bissau 15
Iceland 27
Incas 16
India 5, 21
Jamaica 25
Japan 19, 27
Jolly Roger 26
Kiribati 13
Kuwait 7, 25
Kyrgyzstan 18
Lebanon 13, 25

Malaysia 15, 25
Mexico 17
Middle Ages 6
Nepal 7, 28
Netherlands 10, 12
New Zealand 14, 21
Nigeria 8
North Korea 29
Norway 28, 29
Olympic Games 26
Palau 19
Papua New Guinea 14
Paraguay 12
pennants 6
pennons 6
Peru 16
Red Crescent 26
Red Cross 26
Rome, ancient 5
Russian Federation 12
Saudi Arabia 25
Seychelles 9
Singapore 25
South Africa 21
Spain 10, 12, 16
stars 14–15, 22, 23
Swaziland 17
Switzerland 7
Thailand 25
Turkmenistan 18
Ukraine 8
Union Jack 20–23
United Kingdom 20, 21, 23
United Nations (UN) 24
United States 23, 24, 28